MASTERING 1.9

MINI **HACKS** FOR
MINECRAFTERS

THE UNOFFICIAL GUIDE TO THE COMBAT UPDATE

MEGAN MILLER

Sky Pony Press
New York

Copyright © 2016 by Hollan Publishing, Inc.

Minecraft® is a registered trademark of Notch Development AB.

The Minecraft game is copyright © Mojang AB.

Sky Pony Press books may be purchased in bulk at special discounts for sales
promotion, corporate gifts, fund-raising, or educational purposes. Special editions
can also be created to specifications. For details, contact the Special Sales
Department, Sky Pony Press, 307 West 36th Street, 11th Floor, New York, NY 10018
or info@skyhorsepublishing.com.

Sky Pony® is a registered trademark of Skyhorse Publishing, Inc.®, a Delaware
corporation.

Minecraft® is a registered trademark of Notch Development AB.
The Minecraft game is copyright © Mojang AB.

Visit our website at www.skyponypress.com.

10 9 8 7 6 5 4 3 2

Library of Congress Cataloging-in-Publication Data is available on file.

Cover design by Brian Peterson

Print ISBN: 978-1-5107-1797-8
Ebook ISBN: 978-1-5107-1801-2

TABLE OF CONTENTS

PREFACE

Greetings, fellow Minecrafters! If you haven't played or heard much about Minecraft 1.9, or the Combat Update, yet, here is the big news: We can fly! (Actually, it's gliding, but it's close enough!) We'll look at exactly how to get your wings in this book, and all of the big new features in 1.9, including:

- Your new left hand, and how to use it

- New combat mechanics (a.k.a., click slower)

- How to walk on water

- Crafting an everlasting sword

- The dread skeleton trap

- Igloos and what they hide

- The new Outer End Islands, a weird new mob, and the amazing and rare Elytra wings

Mojang (the creators of Minecraft) also made hundreds of smaller additions, improvements, and tweaks to the game. We'll look at these changes too, so you'll be the master of all 1.9 things and all this release contains!

This book reflects the gameplay added in Minecraft 1.9 (PC). If you are playing a different version of Minecraft, features listed here may not be included or may work a little differently.

CHAPTER 1

DUAL WIELDING

Our lone right arms have been leading the way forward in Minecraft since the beginning. Now with 1.9, if you're a lefty, or if you are up for giving your world double the trouble, you have a whole other hand to use. When you open your inventory, you'll see the new slot for your second hand to the lower right of your character. The slot has an outline of a shield in it, because a new primary ability of wielding with two hands is blocking with a shield. (That's right, you can no longer block with your sword!)

The off-hand slot has the outline of a shield in it.

Main Hands and Off Hands

You can switch which hand is your main or primary hand. Click Options on the Game Menus screen, then click Skin Customization. Click the Main Hand: Right/Left button on the bottom right to toggle which hand is your main hand. Because a player's main hand can be the right or left hand, the non-main hand is called the off hand.

How to Wield Dually: Short Explanation

1. Press F to move an item to your off hand. Proceed.

How to Wield Dually: Long Explanation

1. In your hotbar, select the item you want to go in your off hand. This item should be something with right-click functionality, like a torch that you place with a right-click.

2. Press F to move that item to the off-hand slot. The off-hand slot will appear to the left of your hotbar, if your primary hand is the right hand. If your left hand is your main hand, then the off-hand slot will appear to the right of your hotbar. Of course, you can also press E to open your inventory and drag items to your off-hand slot.

The off-hand slot appears to the left of your hotbar if you've kept the default of using your right hand as your main hand.

3. Scroll or press 1 through 9 to select another item in your hotbar. As usual, the item appears in your main hand, ready to use. This item should be something that doesn't have a right-click functionality, like a pick or a sword (now that swords can't block).

4. Now you can left-click the item in your main hand, and right-click will right-click the item in your off hand.

F will also switch what's in your off hand and main hand.

Unforeseen Consequences

This dual wielding feature can kind of backfire. The game will first look to right-click something in your main hand, and only if that won't work, goes to your off hand for the right click. If whatever is in your off hand breaks or runs out, the game will try to right-click the item in your main hand. Or maybe the item in your main hand only right-clicks in some situations. For example, a shovel doesn't have a right-click function unless it is pointed at a grass block. (See page 81 to read about grass path blocks.)

Or maybe, like me, you haven't been paying much attention to what's in your off hand, or you've mistakenly clicked F. All this means that you can easily wind up spamming blocks or torches around you or just waving your arms about. To avoid this confusion, keep your off-hand slot empty until you have a specific use for it. Here are some great uses:

- **Mining:** Torches in the off hand, pickaxe in your main. This lets you place your torches with a simple right-click as you dig out the precious ores.

- **Blocking and Attacking:** Shield in your off hand, sword (or axe) in your main. See page 8 for more about your new shields and page 31 for using the axe as a weapon.

- **Potions and Attacking:** A potion (or healing milk) in your off hand, sword in your main. This lets you quickly drink a potion in between strikes on your foe.

- **Moving and Attacking:** Ender pearls in your off hand, sword in your main. The Ender pearls let you move fast away from (or sneak up fast to) your enemy in a fight.

- **Seeding a Farm:** Seeds in your off hand and a hoe in your main. (The first right-click hoes the grass block, the second right-click places the seeds.)

- **Growing and Harvesting:** Seeds in your off hand, bone meal in your main. (On hoed land, the first right click places the seed, and the second bone-meals the seed.)

- **Melee and Range:** Bow in your off hand, sword in your main.

- **Healing by Eating:** Food in your off hand, sword in your main.

Dual wielding is for more than just combat—it can come in very handy for farming, as well as mining.

- **Ladder Up:** Building blocks in your off hand, and ladders in your main. Right-click to place the first stone block, and keep right-click pressed. Now you'll automatically switch between your right hand and left hand to create and climb a pillar of stone with attached ladders. This happens because your first right-click (and third, fifth, and so on right-clicks) are at the top of the ground or a just-placed stone block. Your second right-click (and fourth, sixth, and so on right-clicks) are clicking the front side of the stone block you just placed. (This great tip is from YouTuber and Minecraft expert xisumavoid.)

- **Find Your Way:** Map in your off hand, any-thing in your main. You won't be doing any left- or right-clicking with the map, so any right-clicks will apply to what's in your right (main) hand.

Juggle to amuse yourself or your friends.

Juggling: A Very Important Skill

Place a slimeball in your right hand, and nothing in your off hand. Press F5 twice to move to third person view. Now press F rapidly. It looks (a little) like you are juggling! Or, place a redstone torch in one hand and a regular torch in the other. When you press F rapidly, it looks like the torches are lighting up and off!

SHIELDS

Minecraft's brand new shields can protect you from a *lot* of damage from mobs or other players in PvP. They are easy to craft, repair, decorate, and dual wield with weapons. If you've been reading this book from the beginning, you'll know that there is no more blocking with swords. Swords do nothing when you right click them. In 1.9 it is shields that you must use for blocking damage from incoming attacks.

You can use any type of wood planks to craft shields.

You make shields from six wood (any type) and one iron ingot, so they are fairly cheap. They are designed for dual-wielding with a sword or axe in your right or main hand. Place a shield in your off hand when your inventory is open, or click F to move a shield selected in your hotbar to your off hand. When you are attacked, right-click to raise your shield to take the damage, and protect you from:

- 100% of damage from any types of arrows and projectiles, like ghast and blaze fireballs and shulker bullets

- 66% of damage from melee attacks

- Knockback from projectile attacks, such as arrows

- Damage from the Thorns enchantment on opponent's armor

- TNT set off by another player

- Some explosions, like creeper explosions

Shields will protect you from creeper explosions.

A shield won't protect you from any type of potion damage, environmental damage (like fire, suffocation, drowning, or falling), or TNT explosions that you set off yourself or with redstone, and any explosions that don't have an owner (like a Nether crystal or TNT minecart). You can also experience a chance of slight knockback from melee attacks. Also, when you first select your shield, it is disabled for a quarter second before you can use it.

Area of Protection

The shield will protect against attacks coming in from anywhere in the hemisphere in front of you. It doesn't matter whether the attack is off toward the right, left, or straight ahead. It won't protect against any attacks from behind. Arrows you block will sometimes bounce back right to damage the sender, and there is also a chance your shield will knockback your opponent. You can still move while you are right-clicking with a shield, but you'll move slower, at a sneaking pace.

Shields protect you from projectiles like arrows, which bounce right off.

Durability Damage

Your shield starts with 336 points of durability and it will wear down with use. Each attack you block will lower its durability. The number of durability points taken from your shield is the same as the number of damage points of the attack plus 1. So if the incoming melee attack was calculated at 14 points, there would be a total of 15 durability hits on the shield. Remember there are two points for each heart on your heads-up display (HUD). Like weapons and tools, if a shield reaches 0 durability, it will break and disappear. The durability damage done to your armor is calculated after the damage reduction made by your shield, so your shield basically also protects you from damaging your armor. If your shield and armor reduce attack damage to you to less than 1 point, you'll receive no durability loss or damage at all but still get knocked back a bit. And shields won't take any damage if the attack gives less than 3 points of damage (1.5 hearts).

Spiff Up Your Shield

It is easy to decorate your shield by combining it in a crafting grid with a banner. If you don't recall, banners are created with six wool and one stick, and colored with dyes. You can apply different patterns, like stripes, borders, and more by placing the dye in different locations in the crafting grid with your banner. You can add up to six patterns to a banner, one on top of the next.

You can use a banner design to decorate your shield.

There are several popular websites that have banner making tools that make creating banners easier:

- Miners Need Cool Shoes website, at Needcoolshoes.com/banner.

- Planet Minecraft website, at Planetminecraft.com/banner.

At both of these sites you can practice with different layers, colors, and shapes to use in creating banners, before you make the banner in the game. Miners Need Cool Shoes is also a great site for making new skins!

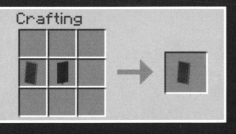

Combine a banner with a shield in a crafting grid to add the banner decoration to the shield.

Repairing Your Shield

There are two ways to repair shields. You can combine two shields in a crafting grid. The repaired shield will have the durability of both shields added together, plus 5 percent. You can also use an anvil to add a block of wood planks to your shield to repair it, for a small enchantment price.

To keep the banner design on a shield, however, you must use an anvil. If you combine a decorated shield with a regular shield on a regular crafting table, you will just get a plain wood shield.

You can place a shield in both hands, but only the one in your main hand will take the damage. This is because dual wielding rules prioritizes the right-click to your main hand. Only when you have a left-click only item in your main hand does the right-click move to the off hand. That said, sporting two shields isn't a bad look!

You can hold two shields at once, but only one will protect you.

Enchanting Shields

You can't enchant a shield with an enchantment table, but you can apply an enchantment with an anvil. There are two enchantments that work with shields, Mending and Unbreakable. For more on the new Mending enchantment, go to page 85.

MORE ARROWS!

Minecraft 1.9 steps up the arrow action by adding fifteen new arrows to your arsenal. That's right, fifteen! That's fourteen tipped arrows and the new spectral arrow. (There's also a new animation in your hotbar showing your bow expanding when you draw an arrow.)

In your hotbar, your arrow is animated to show you drawing your bow.

Tipped Arrows

Tipped arrows are arrows doused with one of the Minecraft potions. They'll affect your victim with the potion's effects, but only up to an eighth of the time the original potion lasted. Here's the catch: The potion you use to create a tipped arrow has to be a lingering potion. A lingering potion is any splash potion that's then been brewed with a bottle of dragon's breath. And to get the dragon's breath, well, you have to fight the Ender Dragon. And fighting the dragon has been made much harder in the 1.9 Combat Update. All this means that you won't be able to make these tipped arrows until you've progressed to what's called the late game. That's when you've gathered enough resources to be able to make potions as well as highly enchanted armor, tools, and weapons, and are ready to do some dragon fighting. For more on dragon's breath, see page 38, and to see how to make a lingering potion, see page 91.

You create eight tipped arrows by surrounding a lingering potion with eight regular arrows. Anyone hit by a tipped arrow will show the same particle effects they'd get if they drank the type of potion used to make the arrow.

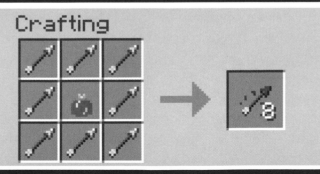

To craft tipped arrows, surround a lingering potion with regular arrows.

The Fourteen New Arrows

Arrow of Fire Resistance	Arrow of Harming
Arrow of Healing	Arrow of Invisibility
Arrow of Leaping	Arrow of Luck*
Arrow of Night Vision	Arrow of Poison
Arrow of Regeneration	Arrow of Slowness
Arrow of Strength	Arrow of Swiftness
Arrow of Water Breathing	Arrow of Weakness

* The arrow of Luck (and the new potion of Luck) is only available in Creative mode. That means it will be mostly used by custom map makers. However, it may someday be brought into Survival mode gameplay. The Luck potion affects how good the loot is that you get from killing mobs, dungeon chests, and fishing.

Spectral Arrows

Shoot an opponent with a spectral (ghostly) arrow, and he or she (or it) will have a glowing outline you can see through other blocks. This glowing status effect will last for 10 seconds. If you are playing on servers with mini-games and teams, the outline will be the color of the opponent's team. Spectral arrows are great for PvP combat when people are hiding behind blocks and structures or using invisibility potions. You craft two spectral arrows at a time by surrounding a regular arrow with four glowstone dust.

 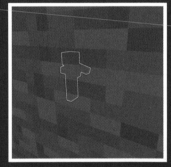

Spectral arrows give your target a glowing outline you can see through blocks.

Arrow Priority

Now that there are more types of arrows, how do you pick which arrows are used when you shoot a bow? Minecraft prioritizes arrows as per their position in your inventory, in the following order:

- Arrows in your dual-wielding slot (the off hand).

- Arrows in your hotbar, starting from the leftmost slot and moving right.

- Arrows in your inventory, starting from the upper left slot moving to the bottom right slot.

The game decides which arrows to shoot based on where they are located in your inventory. Here, the spectral arrow will be shot first, then the orange arrow of fire resistance, followed by the green arrow of leaping, the pink arrow of regeneration, and finally the regular arrows.

Status Effects

In Minecraft 1.8, you could see status effects listed when you opened your inventory. In 1.9, status effect icons are shown on the upper right of your screen. Positive effects (like strength) are listed on a row above negative effects (like poison).

CHAPTER 4

OVERHAULED COMBAT MECHANICS

For years, spam-clicking has been an essential part of Minecraft PvP (and PvMonsters!). Sword in hand, you could conquer many enemies by just clicking as fast as possible with the best sword. With Minecraft 1.9, spam-clicking has been partially nerfed by new weapon mechanics. (*Nerfed* means *debuffed* or made less effective.) Spam-clicking as a tactic means that, on a server, the player with the best speed connecting to the server has an advantage over other players: their spam clicks will fail less and hit more accurately than someone with a slightly laggy connection. Mojang's goal has been to bring in more strategy to combat. This way, players without the best connection and without the best armor and weapons still have a chance to win fights by using better strategy.

What's been changed besides shields? Attack speed, attack damage, armor protection, critical hits, new sword and axe attacks, healing, and more.

Now when you strike a mob, dark hearts will rise up from them. The greater the damage, the more animated hearts you'll see.

Attack Speed

In order for your strike with a weapon to inflict full damage, the weapon must be fully charged. Weapons with high attack speeds recharge faster. You can see the attack speed value of a weapon in the

Advanced Tooltips as you roll over your hotbar or inventory. (If you don't see these tips, press F3+H to turn Advanced Tooltips on.) The higher the attack speed value, the faster the speed of the weapon, and the less time it takes to recharge. A diamond sword has an attack speed of 1.6 while the much slower axe has an attack speed of 1. (The attack speed value doesn't represent the actual speed of your weapon. It is a modifier for a base speed.) The Mining Fatigue effect (from an elder guardian) will slow down your attack speed by 10 percent. The Haste effect (from a beacon) will speed up your attack speed by 10 percent per level.

Attack speed applies to not just swords, but also to axes, pickaxes, hoes, and shovels. Their attack speeds and attack damage are shown on the following pages.

When you roll over a weapon in your inventory, Advanced Tooltips will show its attack speed and damage.

Swords

		ATTACK SPEED	ATTACK DAMAGE
	Diamond Sword	1.6	7
	Gold Sword	1.6	4
	Iron Sword	1.6	6
	Stone Sword	1.6	5
	Wooden Sword	1.6	4

Axes

		ATTACK SPEED	ATTACK DAMAGE
	Diamond Axe	1	9
	Gold Axe	.9	9
	Iron Axe	.8	9
	Stone Axe	1	7
	Wooden Axe	.8	7

Shovels

	ATTACK SPEED	ATTACK DAMAGE
Diamond Shovel	1	5.5
Gold Shovel	1	4.5
Iron Shovel	1	3.5
Stone Shovel	1	2.5
Wooden Shovel	1	2.5

Pickaxes

	ATTACK SPEED	ATTACK DAMAGE
Diamond Pickaxe	1.2	5
Gold Pickaxe	1.2	5
Iron Pickaxe	1.2	3
Stone Pickaxe	1.2	3
Wooden Pickaxe	1.2	2

Hoes

		ATTACK SPEED	ATTACK DAMAGE
	Diamond Hoe	4	1
	Gold Hoe	3	1
	Iron Hoe	2	1
	Stone Hoe	1	1
	Wooden Hoe	1	1

What does this all mean? Well, it means that an axe (if you don't need to swing fast) can do more damage than a sword. And if you take speed into account, you're better off with an iron axe than a diamond axe. Also, if you're out in the fields without your weapons and you are surprise-attacked by a zombie, choose a shovel over a pickaxe to beat it away.

You may also hear this attack speed mechanic referred to as cooldown. Cooldown is the amount of time it takes before the weapon is fully charged, as if it is cooling down to heal. You can still do damage during the cooldown period. The amount of damage that is done depends on how recharged the weapon is, the type of weapon used, and, for axes and hoes, its material. In general, however, the amount of progress in recharging decides the amount of damage. For example, if it takes a diamond sword .6 seconds to recharge, then at .3 seconds it will do about 50 percent of the full 7 hearts of damage, or 3.5 hearts. Immediately after a strike, weapons can do about 20 percent of damage.

Your Attack Indicator

The attack indicator shows how charged your weapons are. To turn the attack indicator on, go to Options and click on Video Settings. Then you can click on the Attack Indicator button to turn on the crosshair or hotbar indicator (or turn it off again.) The crosshair option adds a tiny progress bar below the crosshair. It can be a bit difficult to see. The hotbar option adds a more visible sword icon that fills up like a progress bar to the right of the hotbar. You'll see, with the attack indicator on, that it takes a few moments when you first select a weapon for it to charge up.

(Speaking of crosshairs . . . crosshairs now disappear when you change to third person view by pressing F5. Much better for selfie screenshots!)

The crosshair indicator is a light gray bar right below the center crosshair that can be difficult to see.

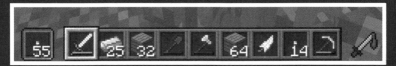

The hotbar attack indicator is a sword icon to the right of the hotbar.

Critical Hits

You can no longer give a critical hit (extra damage) when sprinting. You still have to be falling, but you can't be sprinting, riding something, on a ladder, or in water. You also can't complete a critical hit if you are below about 85 percent of cooldown.

Sword Sweep Attack

The sweep attack works to give damage to multiple foes at once. When you hit a mob with a sword, you also knock back mobs that are close by (within about a block of the attacked mob and three blocks of the attacker—you), along with dealing them 1 point of damage (half a heart). This works only for swords and only if you are still or sneaking (holding shift while moving). A big secondary benefit to the sweep attack is how it affects XP farms. If your farm gathers softened (already damaged) mobs into a small space so that you can one-hit kill them, the sweep attack makes your job much, much easier. In 1.8, you'd have to strike forty one-hit spiders forty times to kill them all. In 1.9, with the sweep attack, you only have to swing a few times.

A sweep attack is animated with a curved white line animation, which you can see here in the bottom right.

The Crushing Blow of the Axe

You axe can now deal what's called a crushing blow to your opponent's shield. If you use an axe to attack someone who's blocking with a shield, there's a 25 percent chance you will disable their shield for five seconds. For each level of Efficiency that your axe has, add 5 percent to that chance of disabling the shield. So if your axe has the Efficiency III enchantment, you have a 40 percent chance (25 percent plus three times 5 percent) of disabling the shield. If you're sprinting while attacking (and your axe is at least 90 percent charged) you will always disable your opponent's blocking shield.

Combat Balancing

In keeping with overhauling the combat system, the Minecraft developers tweaked other related gameplay to rebalance combat. Balancing, in game development, means making sure some aspects of gameplay don't completely overpower others, or that some important gameplay doesn't become irrelevant because of another change or improvement. For example, if a new villager type could trade diamonds for coal, that might mean getting diamonds was now easier than getting coal. To balance that, you'd want to make sure that the villager was very rare, or would only trade one diamond for, say, 500 coal, so that mining was still a needed activity.

In rebalancing combat, the developers have also made changes to:

- **Armor:** Armor is less effective, and damaged armor (with durability loss) protects less. However, armor also has a toughness value, which can reduce the reduction of protection from damaged armor. Diamond armor currently is the only armor with a toughness value.

If armor has a toughness value, it is displayed in the Advanced Tooltips.

- **Potions:** Strengths and lengths have been changed slightly. For example, potions of Strength are weaker, and potions of Weakness are stronger.

- **Enchantments:** Sharpness and Protection enchantments are weaker.

- **Golden Apples:** Regular golden apples are weaker, and enchanted golden apples are no longer craftable. You can only find enchanted golden apples in dungeon chests.

- **Hunger:** Hunger heals you from damage, and you also heal much faster if you eat foods with high saturation. If you are going into battle, put a high saturation food (meat, fish, golden carrots, etc.) on your hotbar so you can eat as you fight.

Watch This Space!

A number of PvP Minecrafters weren't very happy with the first 1.9 release, because it nerfed spam-clicking almost completely. Mojang revised the cooldown mechanics in a following release so that spam-clicking does still inflict some damage. However, Minecraft may continue to make tweaks to combat in the 1.9.X releases and further on down the line.

CHAPTER 5

A NEW END AND A NEW DRAGON

As you know, the End is a large End stone island, floating in a deep purple void. It's been a lonely and stark island, inhabited only by Endermen and the dragon, whom you must defeat in order to "finish" the game. This is still true, except now the End has expanded to include an infinite land of End stone islands and islets called the Outer End Islands. There's a thousand-block wide gap of empty void between the original, central island and the outer islands. (See page 51 for more on the Outer End Islands.) This Combat Update has also upped the ante for the dragon fight. The dragon has been strengthened and a couple more obstacles have been placed on your road to victory.

Destroying the Crystals

You must still break the End crystals atop the obsidian columns, which are now arranged in a circle around an unactivated exit portal. However, now a couple of the shortest obsidian columns have cages of iron bars surrounding their End crystals. This means you cannot shoot them right from the ground like the others. You first have to climb up these pillars and destroy the iron cages, all with a hostile dragon circling. You might also be able to Ender pearl (teleport by throwing an Ender pearl) right to the top of the columns.

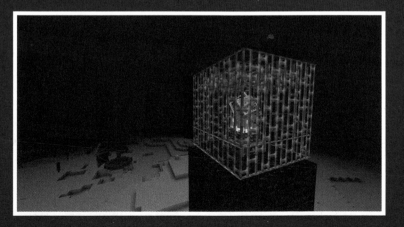

A few End crystals are now protected by iron bars.

Now, an End crystal explosion is still as powerful as a charged creeper and more powerful than a TNT explosion. So you can't break the iron bars around a crystal and then break the crystal right there without taking a fair amount of damage. You can avoid these explosions a couple ways.

- Break all the iron bars, Ender pearl back to the ground, and then shoot arrows at the crystal.

- After you've broken one side of iron bars, use cobblestone to bridge 10 or so blocks away from the crystal and shoot from a distance.

- Place a block of TNT on top of the cage and mosey on out of there. It will take maybe a half minute, but the fire beneath the End crystal will set the TNT alight, causing it to explode and destroy the crystal.

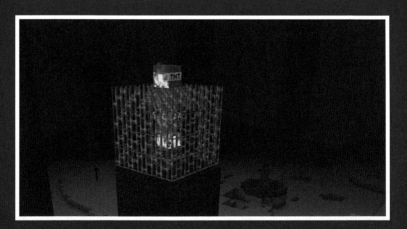

TNT placed on an iron cage will catch fire after a short while.

Also, see how I avoided this explosion damage on page 47.

More End Crystal Breaking Tips:

- Because the dragon interacts with healing crystals, break the iron-caged crystals first. This way, there may be greater odds that the dragon will hover around another crystal while you are at the top of the pillar.

- If your iron-barred crystals are on adjacent columns, it may be faster for you to build a cobblestone bridge to get to the next iron cage. Just keep an eye out for where the dragon is.

- If you destroy a crystal while the dragon is being healed by it, the dragon will take 10 health points (5 hearts) of damage. However, this is really only something to keep in mind with the last crystal you destroy, because until then, there's always another crystal around to heal the dragon.

One Pumped-Up Dragon

Once you've finished off the crystals, you can turn your attention to the dragon. The AI (artificial intelligence) of the Ender Dragon has been upgraded to be more complicated and powerful. (Although a game character's programmed behavior is often called AI, it's not really the same thing as the more complex types of artificial intelligence created and advanced by computer scientists.) The dragon circles outside the ring of obsidian columns, and then inside the columns once all the crystals are destroyed. She will charge at nearby players (like you!). As she charges, she may fire Ender charges at you. This is called the Ender acid attack. These charges are like a fireball, but they are purple, and when they strike, they release a poisonous cloud of dragon's breath particles. The particles spread into a circle about ten blocks wide, and linger on the ground for quite a while. You can end up with many of these pools of harming around you. (Bring a glass bottle to suck up these particles! They are necessary to create the new lingering potions.) She may also charge right at you, knocking you high into the sky with her wings. To survive the fall to the ground, wear Feather Falling IV boots. Or, use Ender pearls to teleport down before you fall, or pour a bucket of water into a pool you can fall into.

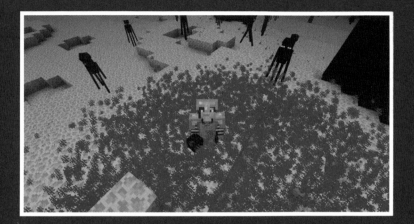

The Ender acid attack results in a cloud of harmful dragon's breath lingering on the ground.

Every so often during her patrol, the dragon flies to her empty bedrock nest in the center of the obsidian columns. She perches above the short bedrock pillar, flapping her wings. And for the five or so seconds that she rests on the nest, she's protected from any arrows. However, you can run up close and hit her with your sword. Be careful though, as she is very likely to spit out her dragon's breath of purple particles. Keep behind her as you sprint up, and be aware of the time—she's only there for a few moments.

The Ender Dragon resting on her perch.

Fighting the Dragon

You'll want to keep moving, to avoid the Ender acid attacks, but it's also hard to fight the dragon as she flies around the obsidian columns. She moves fast and turns often, and most of your arrows will go astray. (And leave the snowballs at home; they no longer damage the dragon.) The best times to shoot her with your arrow are:

- When she is flying directly toward you (or away). Hit her on her head, if you can, because you will inflict full damage on her. Hitting her anywhere else on her body inflicts a quarter of your attack's full damage points.

- Right before she lands on her nest and right after. She's much easier to hit here, just because she is closer.

Resummoning the Dragon

I often felt a little bad, killing the only dragon alive in my world. Even though, really, she is just pixels in a videogame, the dragon made me think of endangered and magnificent Earth creatures. Well, if you are like me, then you can feel a bit better. The Ender Dragon is no longer a one-time event. You can resummon the dragon, for another fight, or just to have around for an occasional scare.

To resummon the dragon, place four End crystals on the outer edges of the exit portal.

To resummon the dragon, you will need four End crystals. And in 1.9, you can now craft these, using an Eye of Ender, a ghast tear, and seven glass blocks. Place an End crystal in the center of each of the four sides of the nest, and a dramatic light and explosion show, rivaling the dragon's death, will start. Light beams from the four placed crystals focus together on each obsidian pillar in turn. At each pillar, the beams bring forth a new healing crystal with a powerful explosion. Once all the crystals are reborn, beams of light from each crystal converge in the sky, and with an even more powerful explosion, a new Ender Dragon is born above the nest.

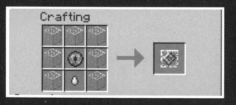

End crystals can be crafted now with glass, a ghast tear, and an Eye of Ender.

You can resummon the dragon up to twenty times. Once the dragon is resummoned, the exit portal back to the Overworld is also reset—you'll only be able to teleport back when you've killed her.

A dramatic laser spectacle comes with the resummoning of the dragon.

More about End Crystals

- End crystals can only be placed on top of obsidian or bedrock. They're one of the few blocks in Minecraft that can't be destroyed by a dragon.

- They heal the dragon one health point (half a heart) for each half second that she's within thirty-two blocks.

- They explode easily—any attack on them, from an arrow or a snowball, will cause them to detonate.

- Although you can craft End crystals in the Overworld, you can only respawn an Ender Dragon with the End exit portal.

Why Is the Dragon a She?

Well, the dragon lays an egg. That's one pretty big reason. Also, the creator of Minecraft, Notch, or Marcus Persson, said in a public discussion forum that "She's from the End," and that her name was "Jean?" Notch also named Minecraft's Steve on Twitter in a similar way: "And I tend to always put a question mark after his name (Steve?)."

The Deaths of the Dragons

The dragon's death is pretty much the same spectacular light show as before. One difference is that the dragon flies back toward the exit portal before dying (that's where she drops off her egg). The first dragon to die will leave her egg and 12,000 XP worth of experience orbs. After this, resummoned dragons will only leave 500 XP and no egg. However, with each of these deaths, the dragon will leave a new portal to the Outer End Islands. Each new portal leads to a new area of the islands, which you can read more about on page 52.

CHAPTER 6

HOW I BEAT THE ENDER DRAGON

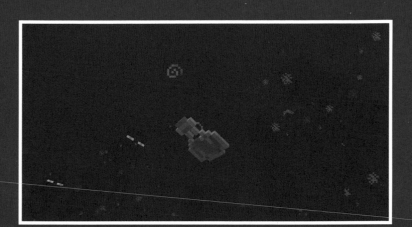

I can't claim to be the best swordsperson or have the greatest aim. You might call me "cautious" and I tend to swing wildly if I'm surprised by an attack. Maybe it's 50-50 that I panic and end up throwing my weapons at my opponent. However, with all this, I still beat the Ender Dragon by myself, in a single-person world. It did take me what felt like an hour, and two deaths. Here's how I did it: I used the Invisibility potion and no armor!

My first visit to the End was with fully enchanted diamond armor and potions and it resulted in my being constantly pummeled by the dragon, even through the obsidian shelters I created. There was so much pummeling I could barely think. So much I forgot to not look at the Endermen, and had to flee and fight them several times. The dragon threw me into the air several times (to my death), clouded me with its Ender acid breath, and just plain beat me.

I was also thrown into the sky by the incredible knockback that came with the dragon's massive body-slam.

For my second attempt, I decided to try the Invisibility potion. In previous versions, this hasn't always worked so well for me. Somehow the mobs and the boss mobs always saw me. This time, however, armorless, I found myself fully invisible. When I got to the End, the dragon completely ignored me!

I gazed skyward as I waltzed through the throngs of Endermen toward the center of the island. Looking up kept my cursor above them and prevented myself from accidentally angering them. (I actually did fail at this a couple more times, and used up most of my potions of Healing and Regeneration recovering from these skirmishes.)

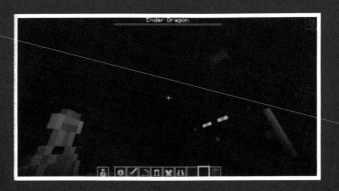

Keeping your cursor high in the screen helps you avoid looking at the Endermen's bodies and aggravating them.

As I walked, I located the shorter pillars that had the iron cages on them. I used the stack of sand I brought to pillar quickly up the side of these short columns with iron cages. Two blocks from the top, I used my pick to break the bottom corner of the iron cage. Then I could reach inside the cage and break the crystal with my pick. There was a huge explosion, but I was completely protected by the obsidian on two sides of me.

This is where I stood to smash the caged crystals and avoid the explosion. In the actual fight, though, I was invisible.

I used my OP (overpowered) Efficiency V shovel to break my sand pillar and get back to the ground. Then it was time to use bow and arrow to shoot the other crystals, the ones that were unprotected by iron cages. And remember, all this time, I'm invisible—the Ender Dragon is circling the columns, but it isn't charging straight at me. It did get close a couple times, just 'cause we were both moseying around the same area, and I was killed once more. Its wings knocked me high into the sky, and I died by hitting the ground.

After this death, and after breaking all the crystals, I moved close, about twenty blocks, from the bedrock exit portal. This is where the dragon rests in between its flights around the columns. Now, you can't shoot the dragon with arrows while it is resting here, because some kind of invisible fiery force field repels the arrows. However, you CAN hit the dragon just before it stops and just after it resumes its flight and this is one of the easiest times to hit it, because it's close. This is where I got 99 percent of my hits on the dragon in. A couple of times the dragon released its poisonous breath particles, but I was far enough away that I was able to easily keep safe.

This is how close I stood to shoot the dragon just before and after she rested on the perch.

And that was it. It took maybe twenty shots that hit and 200 shots that didn't with my Power V Infinity bow. It was a fairly long time hanging around the center, avoiding looking at Endermen, checking my status effects to see when to drink the next Invisibility potion, and shooting at the dragon when it came to rest.

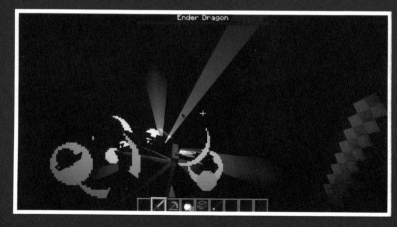

The final death of the dragon.

CHAPTER 7

TRAVELING TO THE OUTER END ISLANDS

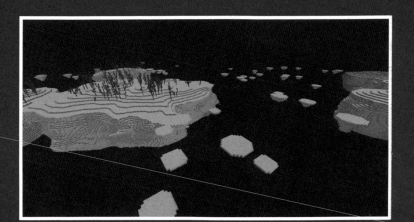

To get to these new lands in Minecraft you need to first defeat the dragon. When the dragon dies, it leaves not just the working exit portal, but another portal floating in the air. This is called the End gateway portal, and you'll typically find it about seventy blocks away from the island center. When it first appears, the portal emits a purplish beam above and below it. Look for this when you kill the dragon.

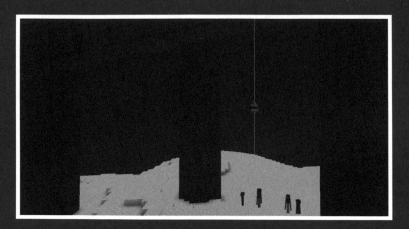

The purple beam at the portal only appears for a few moments after the death of the dragon.

Like the exit portal, the portal to the Outer End Islands is made of bedrock. These are much smaller and are just a few blocks of bedrock above and below a space-warpy block that looks like the middle of an activated End portal.

Once you've located the End gateway portal, you'll likely have to build a bridge or stairway to it. And you can't walk through the portal, because it is only one block. You throw an Ender pearl through it and that will teleport you to the Islands. There, you may land on a larger islands or one of the many small islands. If you're on a small island, you'll need blocks to build bridges to larger islands. If you're good at Ender pearling, you can use Ender pearls to jump between closer islands.

The new End gateway portal hovers in the air, so you'll have to build or Ender pearl up to it.

How to Get to the End Islands Without Killing the Dragon

If you have incredible patience, you can build a thousand block bridge out from the central islands. It took me a full fifteen minutes of sneaking backward (with Invisibility potions), placing obsidian blocks, and then cobblestone one block at a time, to travel the 1,060 or so blocks to the Outer End Islands. I just barely had enough blocks to get to a small island. On the small island, I had to mine a stack and a half of End stone to make a bridge to the nearest big island. Getting back was about twice as fast, but I did aggro (make aggressive) an Endermen when I was just twenty blocks from the main island. That Enderman dispatched me into the void quickly and prematurely, with very little sympathy for my arduous journey.

Building a thousand-block bridge to the Outer End Islands is not impossible!

Fly Me to the End

There's a popular redstone contraption you can build to get to the outer islands. It's not too difficult to build, but it is slow, so you won't get to the islands much faster than building a bridge. That said, it is a fun and simple build. And theoretically, you could set yourself up in this flying contraption, then go do something for ten minutes while you're flying, and come back to commandeer your arrival at the outer islands. To make this contraption, you need two pistons, one sticky piston, three blocks of redstone, and two slime blocks. You'll also need some extra helper blocks to help you place these blocks in the right location, including a platform to stand on.

1. Two blocks above the ground, or away from the island, place a regular piston that faces away from the island. Since the Outer End Islands form a doughnut-like ring around the center island, any direction you choose is fine.*

2. Place a slime block in front of the piston, as shown.

* Here, and with other steps, you'll have to place temporary helper blocks in order to place certain blocks. To keep these steps clear, I haven't shown these helper blocks.

3. Place a sticky piston facing into the slime block and toward the island, as shown.

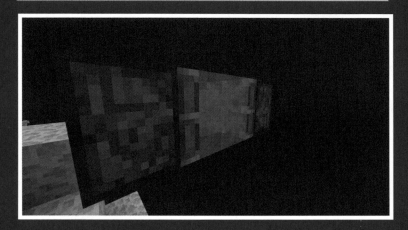

4. On the other side of the sticky piston, place another regular piston, again facing away from the island.

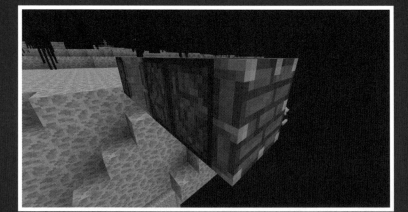

5. Place a slime block on the front of the regular piston.

6. Now place a redstone block on top of each of the two slime blocks.

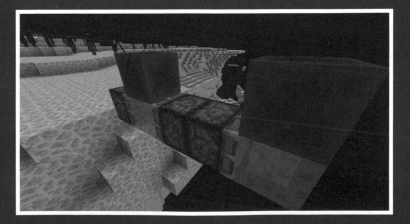

7. Finally, place a redstone block on top of the second regular piston (the one that is furthest from the island). The contraption will expand. Stand on top of this redstone or the piston behind it.

8. Now break this last redstone block. The contraption will start extending and closing, the slime blocks and pistons pulling themselves along.

9. You can stop the contraption by placing a redstone block again on the second regular piston, and restart it by breaking that redstone block. Also, when this flying contraption reaches an End stone block on an island, it will stop.

You'll know when you are close at the Outer End Islands because you'll see the islands instead of the dark purple void. A lot of these islands are barely platforms; you'll want to make your way to one of the larger islands, as that is where the good stuff is.

CHAPTER 8

EXPLORING THE OUTER END ISLANDS

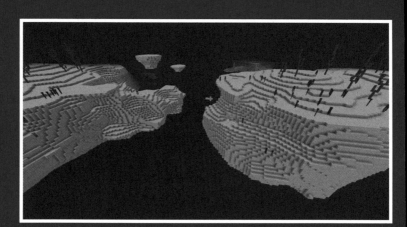

Remember to bring plenty of blocks for building bridges and Ender pearls for teleporting. As in the Nether, you're not going to be able to use a bed (it will explode) and set a spawn or use a compass. To make sure you find your way around, keep a tab on your portal's XYZ coordinates location through the debug (F3) screen. Because you may be traveling far, bring an Ender chest to store your loot in (and a Silk Touch pick to break the chest).

The Chorus Plant

The first thing you'll see when you arrive at the Outer End Islands are the tall new fruit—the chorus plants. They can grow up to about twenty blocks high, and they're purple, in keeping with the general color theme of the End. As they grow, they branch out like trees.

To harvest their fruit, break the bottom block. The chorus plant will break from the bottom to the top in a satisfying chain-reaction of popping sounds.

To grow new chorus plants, you'll need to use a chorus flower as a seed. The chorus flowers grow at the tops of all the branches of the plant. They are a bit bigger than the regular plant blocks of the stem, and have a little yellowish (End stone yellow) circle in the center of each side. These flowers won't drop when you break a stem block; you have to break them individually. You don't need Silk Touch—a regular pick or axe will do. To plant, just place a chorus flower on End stone. You can do this in the Overworld, too, as long as you use End stone instead of dirt.

Chorus flowers are slightly larger blocks at the tops of chorus plant branches.

You can eat that chorus fruit if you are hungry—it will give you four hunger points and a little saturation. However, it can also randomly teleport you up to thirty-two blocks away, in just the way Endermen teleport. If you're close to the edge of an island, or a cliff in the Oveworld, you could be teleported right over the edge. (If you're in a pickle though, it might come in handy!)

You can also smelt chorus fruit—this will produce popped chorus fruit. You can't eat these, but you can craft four of them together to create a new 1.9 decorative block, the purpur block.

Smelting chorus fruit creates popped chorus fruit.

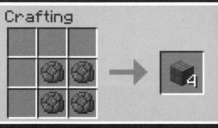

Four popped chorus fruit creates four purpur blocks.

The Purpur Block

Craft four popped chorus fruit in a square to create a purpur block (*purpur* is a Swedish word for purple). Three purpur blocks will make a purpur slab, and six will make purpur stairs. You can also create a purpur pillar block by crafting two purpur slabs.

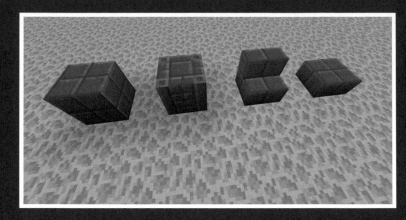

The four new purpur blocks – standard, pillar, stairs, and slabs.

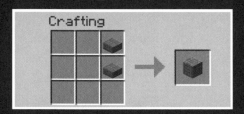

Craft the purpur pillar block from two purpur slabs.

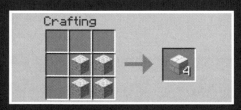

You use four End stone to craft End stone bricks.

End Stone Bricks

End stone bricks are another new block that the 1.9 brings. Craft four End stone blocks in a square to create them.

End Cities

Once you've had your fill of the chorus plant, and snagged some fruit and flowers for your loot collection, you will want to look for an End city. End cities are where you will find the most epic loot of the game. They are dungeonlike structures. They're called dungeonlike because they are a labyrinth (elaborate and mazelike) structure. They are generated in a similar, somewhat random way as Minecraft's strongholds and Nether fortresses, which are other dungeon structures. However, End cities are all aboveground. You'll have no problem recognizing them—they are tall towers of purpur blocks and End stone brick, decorated with black and purple banners. Smaller End cities will be a single tower; larger ones will have multiple towers branching off the central tower.

You can, however, have a hard time finding them. They are not common, and you can potentially travel a thousand blocks in one direction without finding any. To increase your odds of discovering one, change your render distance. The render distance decides how many chunks (16x16 block sections of the world) from your location will be shown in your game screen. To change render distance, open your Options screen, select Video Settings, and move the Render Distance slider to the right. The greater the render distance, the greater strain on your computer graphics, so be aware that if you have big problems with rendering (graphics being drawn), you will want to shorten the distance.

You can change the render distance up to thirty-two chunks—at this distance, your graphics will draw more slowly. However, stopping and looking in all the directions around you will make it easier to find a city.

A very small End city, with one wider tower above the narrow tower.

End cities will have different combinations of purpur bridges and stairs branching to short towers of rooms and longer purpur towers. The towers have Parkour-type stairs inside them—the narrow towers have blocks winding upward that are easy to jump up. The wide towers have greater gaps between the staircase blocks, and more difficult blocks to jump on. These are the End rods, a narrow block like a stick that emits light, which you can also jump onto.

End Rods

End rods are the torches of End cities. They emit a light level 14, like torches, and you will find them inside and outside the cities. You can craft them yourself, using one blaze rod atop a popped chorus fruit. You can stack End rods end to end in a column. Two End rods join together with their bases at either end.

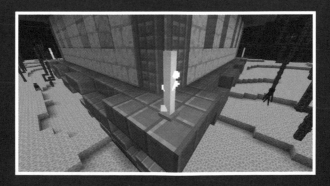

You can find the new sparkling light block, the End rod, at End cities.

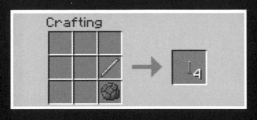

You can craft End rods with one blaze rod and one popped chorus fruit.

Inside the End Cities: Loot and Shulkers

There are two main things you will find inside an End city: chests with fantastic loot and the shulkers. The fantastic loot may be armor, tools, and weapons, with high levels of enchantments, as well as horse armor, emeralds, iron, gold, diamonds, and saddles. (And maybe some beetroot seeds.) The shulkers are brand new mobs, the guardians of the End cities. Read more about them in the next section.

THE SHULKER

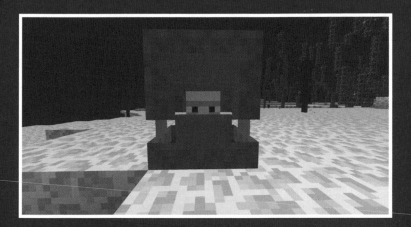

The shulkers are guardians of the End city, and you'll find them at the ground floor entrance, as well as inside the towers, at the tops of towers, and protecting chests, and sometimes even outside the towers and on top of roofs. One of the End cities' wide towers that I saw had twelve shulkers, up and down the inside walls. At the top room of that tower, though, two chests contained a very well-enchanted iron helmet and leggings, eight iron ingots, thirteen diamonds, and diamond pants with Blast Protection IV. Not too shabby!

The narrow towers have slabs you can jump between to climb up, or you can place blocks between them to make a staircase.

The wider towers have blocks placed so that you can jump up around the walls, but it's much more difficult Parkour than the narrow towers. And shulkers line the walls. Here you can see bullets firing past

The name *shulker* is short for "shell lurker," and these mobs hide in a one-block cubed armored purple shell that looks very much like an ordinary purpur block. They are stationary and attach themselves to solid blocks. They are well camouflaged against the purpur walls and floors of the End cities, so you'll need to keep a sharp lookout for them. Every so often the shell opens, and inside you can see a small face. (Lob a splash potion of Invisibility at the shulker—this will hide its shell so you can just see the face.)

Two shulkers are attached to the walls outside the entrance of End cities.

The shulker will start tracking and attacking you when you are about sixteen blocks away, right around when you can start to hear its belching and croaking sounds. When it begins its attack, its upper shell raises and spins. Then it fires projectiles at you that follow you as you move. If other shulkers are nearby, they'll start firing at you too. The projectiles are called bullets and travel only along the x, y, and z axes in straight lines, and take right angles to change course. You can attack the bullets to destroy them, but if they hit you, they'll cause four points of damage. The bullets also give you a levitation effect that lasts ten seconds. You'll start floating in the air, and after ten seconds drop to the ground. Levitating this way, inside an End city tower, isn't necessarily the worst thing in the world, and you can just ride the effect to the next level. But you don't have a lot of control over it, and you need to make sure you aren't too far away from the ground when you drop. You can also counteract the levitation effect by eating a chorus fruit, but you don't have much control over where that teleports you to. It can be safer to use an Ender pearl to teleport to the ground.

Ender bullets can change direction and follow straight lines along the x, y, and z axes.

Here are some interesting facts about shulkers:

- Like Endermen, they don't like water and will teleport somewhere else (but nearby) if you pour water on them.

- They can also teleport short distances when they are damaged.

- Shulkers are strong—stronger than zombies and skeletons. They have thirty health points (fifteen hearts), and their armor is also very strong. Your attacks against them will be more effective if you strike when their shells are open. In fact, arrows won't hurt their closed shells at all.

- They can be caught by each other's bullets and start attacking each other.

CHAPTER 10

END SHIPS AND THE ELYTRA

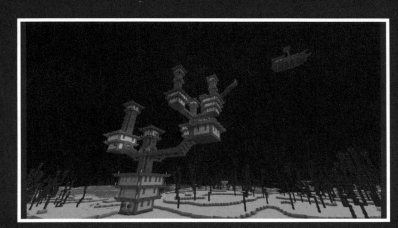

When you find an End city, look for an End ship. This is your ultimate goal in the Outer End Islands. At some End cities, you will find a purpur and End stone airship floating away from a city bridge. This is an End ship, and its loot includes the grand prize of the End—the Elytra. The Elytra is a set of wings (they look a bit like bug wings, more than bird wings) that will let you glide through the air. To get them, you'll have to build a crossing to the End ship (or Ender pearl there) and battle the shulkers protecting the ship.

The End ships always face from away what looks like a launching gate.

In the treasure room, behind the chests and the shulker, is an item frame holding the Elytra.

Inside, there are two main rooms. In one you'll find a brewing stand with two potions of Healing. In the second, lower room you'll find the loot: two chests protected by a shulker, and behind them, an item frame holding the rare Elytra. Once you've defeated the shulker and retrieved this loot, don't leave the ship yet. Make your way to the bow (front) of the ship, where a dragon's head is attached. Right now, this is the only way to get a dragon's head.

The dragon's head is attached to the bow of the End ship.

Dragon's Head

You can wear the dragon's head. As you walk, the mouth will open and close. You can also apply a redstone signal to the head the make the mouth open and close.

The Elytra

To use the Elytra, place them in your chestplate armor slot. To activate the wings, you need to press the spacebar (jumping) right after you jump off a high spot. You'll be gliding! You can glide a little amount up, by looking upward, and you'll move faster pointing downward. According to the Minecraft wiki, you'll glide the longest in the air by pointing just a little bit upward. Look left and right to move left and right. Since the wings are unpowered, you can't fly upward much, or fly forever, and you can't end up higher than where you started.

As you fly, the wings take durability damage. The Elytra have 431 durability, and you have a total of about seven minutes of gliding before you'll need to repair them. Happily, they won't disappear when they lose all durability. You repair them with leather using an anvil. You can also enchant your wings with Mending and with Unbreaking.

The Elytra wings look a lot like a cape when you are not flying.

Elytra wings are gray, although if you have a cape (from attending a Minecon event), the wings will take on the pattern of your cape. While you are flying, you are positioned horizontally, so you take vertically less than a full space. If you get good at gliding, you can actually fit through a one-block space.

NEW GAMEPLAY

In addition to the updates to combat and the End, the Minecraft 1.9 update brings a ton of new content, from new blocks and buildings to a new surprise enemy—the skeleton trap.

The Skeleton Trap

If you hear a thunderstorm, you may want to stay inside. But if you want to witness the incredible skeleton trap, stay outside. In 1.9, a lightning bolt has a chance to spawn a single skeleton horse. If you play on Easy, the chance is lower, and if you play on Hard difficulty, the chance is greater, up to about one in three. That single horse is the skeleton trap. If you or another player gets close, within ten blocks, another bolt of lightning will strike the skeleton horse, transforming it into four skeleton horses with skeleton riders. The skeleton riders wear enchanted helmets and hold enchanted bows. These deadly skeleton horsemen are protected from being damaged in the first few seconds, and they are very fast.

Once you dispatch their riders (don't kill the horses!) skeleton horses are like regular horses, just very bony. They are already tamed, and you can put a saddle on them and ride them. You can't put horse armor on them though, but they are pretty fearsome without that!

Grass Paths

There's a brand new way to make roads in Minecraft, and that's with the grass path block. You create the grass path block by right-clicking a grass block with a shovel (you can't pick it up with a Silk Touch weapon). Grass path blocks combine to form wider paths, whose center is a bit lighter or more golden than the edges. The grass path block is actually a tiny bit shorter than a full block, at 15/16 of one block. In addition to making great rustic paths, this block is also great to make the edges of ponds or the middle of pigsties a bit muddy, or may be combined with other blocks for a partly trodden effect on a path.

The new grass path block you create by right-clicking with a shovel.

You can use the grass path block for more than paths—it's a good way to make ground uneven or look muddy.

Igloos

Igloos—they're cold, white, and round (Minecraft "round")! You'll find them in cold, snowy biomes—the Ice Plains and Cold Taiga. They're made of snow blocks and have windows at the sides made of ice and a doorless entryway. Inside you'll find a cozy single room with carpeting, crafting table, a redstone torch for dim light, and a furnace. They make a great pit stop if you are traveling. Some igloos (about half) will also hide a secret. At the back of the interior, hidden beneath carpet, is a trapdoor, which leads to a hidden dungeon room. Here are two jailed villagers, one regular and one zombie. In this dungeon room also is a brewing stand, a chest, a cauldron, and a clay pot with cactus. Inside the chest and in the brewing stand are a golden apple and a splash potion of Weakness, the cure for the zombie villager.

Igloos can be hard to spot in the snowy biomes so keep an eye out for their distinctive shape.

Boats

Boats are fixed! They no longer break when you sail by a lily pad or brush up against the shore, and they have become a great way to get around. (It seems to me that rivers are a bit wider, longer, and easier to travel too, but this could just be my imagination.) In addition, boats:

- Have paddles

- Go faster than 1.8 boats and go really fast on ice!

- Can carry two entities (you just need to ride a boat near a mob or push them into the boat)

- Have six varieties, for each type of wood

- Move by using the WASD keys (A and D spin you to the left or right)

- Try to put you on the nearest land block you are looking at, when you press Shift to disembark

- Can no longer travel upward vertically in water

- Can be driven on land, slowly

Boats move much faster now and break much less.

Beetroot

There's a new veggie in town and it's a red beetroot. You can find beetroot growing in villages and find their seeds in chests. You grow and harvest them in the same way as other vegetables. Six beetroot on top of a wooden bowl make beetroot soup, and you can craft a single beet into the rose red dye. Roses can be hard to come by, so it's nice to have another way to make red dye. You can use beetroot to lure and breed pigs. (You can also now use potatoes to breed pigs.) Eating a beetroot gives you 1 hunger and just a little saturation; eating beetroot soup restores 6 hunger points and 7.2 points of saturation.

You can find the pinkish-red beetroot growing in villages.

New Enchantments—Frost Walker and Mending

There are two new enchantments in 1.9, Frost Walker and Mending. These are special "treasure" type of enchantments—you won't be able to find them using your enchanting table. You'll have to look for them in chests, fish them up, or trade with villagers for them. Trading with villagers is probably your best bet.

Frost Walker is a boot enchantment and it turns source blocks of water to ice, in a circle around you, and lets you walk on water. The water turns into a special type of ice, frosted ice, which melts fairly quickly in daylight back into water. The frosted ice won't harm squid or other stuff in the water, it will just avoid those inhabited blocks. Frost Walker I turns water blocks within two blocks of you to ice, and Frost Walker III turns water to ice within three blocks of you. You have to start off on ground for this to work; if you jump off a cliff with Frost Walker boots into the sea, no ice will be formed. Also, Depth Strider and Frost Walker are mutually exclusive: you can't have (in Survival mode) both enchantments on the same boots.

The Frost Walker enchantment on your boots lets you walk on water!

The Mending enchantment is kind of a game changer when it comes to enchanting your tools, weapons, shields, and armor. Mending lets your stuff be repaired by experience points that you are currently gathering from an activity. Specifically, each point of XP will undo two points of durability. As you kill mobs, mine ore, and smelt things in the furnace, the XP orbs that usually fill up your XP bar will first go toward gear enchanted with Mending. The gear must be in one of six slots—the four armor slots, the new off-hand/shield slot, and the currently selected hotbar slot (what's in your main hand). Once your mending gear is repaired, the XP will go back to filling up your XP bar. If you have more than one item enchanted with Mending, the game will randomly choose what item to repair. (If you want to specifically repair one item, then make sure that's the only item you are using or wearing.) This means that your perfect enchanted sword (especially combined with the Unbreaking enchantment) will last much, much longer.

TWEAKS AND UPDATES

In addition to the big-ticket additions to the game—combat, the End, igloos, and more—there are a ton of smaller additions and changes.

Mob Behavior

Overall, mobs are harder to fight and kill. Mob AI (artificial intelligence) has been improved, and mobs are smarter about finding their way (pathfinding) around water and potential dangers. For example:

- Mobs can find water if they are on fire, walk over lily pads, and more.

- Endermen move faster, and don't give up if they take water or other damage.

- Skeletons move a lot faster, and they can move sideways AND shoot you. If you go after them, they'll move back a little so they can keep shooting you. If you move back, they'll move forward. They're faster on the draw. Battle them with your shield to block their arrows. After they shoot, strike with your sword, raise your shield, and repeat.

Other mob behavior changes include:

- Zombies raise their arms when they start tracking you. Zombie pigmen do this too.

- Hostile mobs fight each other. If a skeleton accidentally hits another skeleton, the two will target each other.

- Skeletons and zombies can dual wield now, and they have a small chance of spawning left-handed.

- Most mobs and players can push each other now. The pushes you can give and receive aren't extreme, but you will be bounced around a bit in a pen filled with cows.

- Wearing a hostile mob head (zombies, creepers, skeletons), which you can get by mobs dying as a result of a charged creeper explosion, will reduce the detection range of the mob whose head you are wearing by 50 percent. This stacks with sneaking and invisibility. So if a zombie starts tracking you at forty blocks, then wearing a zombie head will lessen this to twenty blocks.

Potions

There've been a number of changes to potions and brewing. Brewing potions has been made a bit more difficult. You now have to add blaze powder to the stand in order to brew any potions. One blaze powder will last for twenty brewing sessions, whether you brew one, two, or three bottles in a session. Other changes include:

- **Splash Potions of Water:** You can now brew a splash water bottle using one gunpowder and bottles of water and throw it at fire to put it out. The splash potion can extinguish fire on one block and up to four more of the adjacent blocks.

Standing in a lingering potion of Luck.

- **Lingering Potions:** Like splash potions, lingering potions are regular potions that can be thrown from your hand or a dispenser. Unlike splash potions, lingering potions create a small puddle of potion particles that stay on the ground for about thirty seconds. During that time, the puddle of potion weakens and the puddle decreases in size. Lingering potions are used to craft the new tipped arrows (see page 18). You brew lingering potions in the same way you brew splash potions. Instead of using gunpowder as the agent in the top slot, you use a bottle of dragon's breath. To get the dragon's breath, you'll have to go to the End, of course (see page 38).

- **Luck Potion:** You can't get or brew the Luck potion in survival mode (at least not yet), but it has been added to creative mode and is usable by map makers. It gives you better chances of getting better loot in chests, while fishing, and by killing mobs.

- **Potion Rebalancing:** Along with changes to combat to make it generally harder, potions have been tweaked so that they offer fewer advantages to potion users. The potion of Strength is not as powerful, and the potion of Weakness is more powerful.

New Command Blocks

There are two new command blocks for map makers and techies. One, the repeat command block, will repeat the command you enter continuously. The other, the chain command block, won't perform its command until a command block that faces it performs its own command. To create these new blocks, press the "Impulse" button in the command block interface to toggle among the three choices: Impulse (normal), Repeat, and Chain.

Command blocks change color depending on whether they are standard (left), chain (middle), or repeat (right).

In additional, you can set a command block to be conditional by toggling the unconditional/conditional button in the interface. A conditional command will only perform its command if there is a command block behind it that executed its own command successfully. (In unconditional mode, there is no such restriction.) You can also set a command block to require redstone activation in order to perform its command.

Set Console Command for Block

Console Command

Use "@p" to target nearest player
Use "@r" to target random player
Use "@a" to target all players
Use "@e" to target all entities

0

| Impulse | Unconditional | Needs Redstone |

| Done | Cancel |

In the new command block interface, you select the type of command it is, and specify whether it is conditional or needs redstone.

Overall, the Minecraft game developers fixed close to 400 bugs and made lots of performance enhancements and minor tweaks, to improve performance, gameplay, and graphics. These include:

- **Bunnies:** Bunnies are smaller and much weaker (1.5 hearts) and run faster. If you get within eight blocks of them, they'll panic and run from you.

- **Dead bushes:** Dead bushes drop sticks when you break them.

- **Doors:** You can click to one side of a block or the other to make a door's hinges attach on that side of the block. (When you are making double doors, though, the hinge will be placed so that the two doors open in the center.)

- **Ender pearls:** Ender pearls have a cooldown period. This means that after throwing one, you can't throw another for a few moments.

- **Hay bales:** Hay bales can reduce your fall damage by 80 percent. You can actually fall 100 blocks without armor and survive (just barely)!

- **Iron bars and glass panes:** The appearance of single iron bars and single glass panes has been changed to show a thin single column now instead of four narrow sides.

- **Iron golems:** Iron golems don't take knockback from hostile mobs, so they are more able to fight zombies and skeletons.

- **Rain:** It rains less!

- **Shears:** Shears are no longer enchantable with Silk Touch and you no longer need Silk Touch to make cobwebs drop cobwebs instead of string.

- **Sleeping:** Sleeping graphics have changed so that you can now see your boots and items in your hand when you lie in bed.

- **Sneaking:** When you sneak and walk (press Shift while walking) you'll use half the energy you do when walking regularly.

- **Snow golems:** You can use shears to remove a snow golem's pumpkin head to reveal a funny, sweet, snow person face below.

- **Sounds:** Many, many new sounds were added, and not just to new gameplay. Some of the best are the witches' cackles—they really help warn you ahead of time that a witch is nearby. Furnaces also make a little sizzling sound now.

- **Strongholds:** There used to be just three strongholds in a world; now there are 128.

- **Trapdoors:** Trapdoors can now stand alone; they don't need to be attached to a block.

- **Villagers:** Cleric villagers don't sell Eyes of Ender any more, but they will sell you Ender pearls to make them with.

- **XP orbs:** XP orbs used to float up to your head. Now you will absorb the orbs around your middle.

Zombie villagers now dress in zombified versions of their professional clothes.

MORE HACKS FOR MINECRAFTERS

Check out other unofficial Minecrafter
tips and tricks from Sky Pony Press!

Hacks for Minecrafters
MEGAN MILLER

Hacks for Minecrafters:
Master Builder
MEGAN MILLER

Hacks for Minecrafters:
Combat Edition
MEGAN MILLER

Hacks for Minecrafters:
Redstone
MEGAN MILLER

Hacks for Minecrafters:
Command Blocks
MEGAN MILLER

Hacks for Minecrafters:
Mods
MEGAN MILLER